LUTHER BURBANK
NATURE'S HELPER

LUTHER BURBANK

NATURE'S HELPER

LILLIAN J. BRAGDON

Illustrated by Frederick T. Chapman

Nashville   **ABINGDON PRESS**   *New York*

ISBN 0-687-22872-7

To Betty and Ed
whose green thumbs created beauty
in my garden

CONTENTS

LUTHER BURBANK
NATURE'S HELPER

CHAPTER ONE

· A GREAT DISCOVERY ·

It had been a long cold winter. Luther was tired of the heavy blanket of snow that covered the fields and roads. He hated to stay cooped up in the house. So he decided to go out exploring in spite of the snow. Wrapping up warmly, he started out in search of something different.

What he found was so exciting he could hardly wait to get home to tell about it. He could hardly believe he hadn't dreamed it all. He hoped Cousin Levi would be there. Cousin Levi had an important job at the Museum of Natural Science in Boston. He knew more about everything than anyone Luther had ever met.

The family was about to sit down when Luther arrived. And Cousin Levi was there. Washing his hands quickly, Luther joined the family. He was so full of excitement that he forgot he was hungry.

As soon as supper had been served, he exclaimed, "What do you think I saw in the woods this afternoon?"

"A bear?" asked his younger brother, Alfred.

"A pussycat?" asked four-year-old Emmy.

"Tell us, son," said his father.

"Yes, tell us," said Cousin Levi.

"Well," Luther began, "I was walking through the snow when suddenly I saw . . . what do you think?" He paused and looked about the table, then went on. "I saw some tall green grass, some beautiful bushes, and . . ." Luther paused again as he got ready to tell the best part. "And I saw some butter-cups growing in the snow."

"Huh, is that all?" said Alfred, disappoint-ed. "That's nothing."

"Buttercups?" cried Emmy. "Did you pick them for me? I didn't know there were butter-cups in the snow."

"Neither did I," said Luther. "I couldn't believe my eyes. I thought I was dreaming. Plants and flowers just don't grow in the snow. I kneeled down to look at them, and what do you think? There was a warm spring coming up from between the rocks. The rocks were covered with a bright green moss, too. And all around there was ice and snow!"

Luther turned eagerly to Cousin Levi.

"Was it because of the warm water that the plants could grow?" he asked. "Did you know that there were warm springs in the woods?"

"Of course I did," Cousin Levi answered.

"I even wrote an article about the warm springs in this part of the valley. I'll read it to you the next time I come. I'm glad you discovered this for yourself, Luther. Now you know that where there is warm air or warm water, plants that cannot stand ice and snow can grow even in winter."

"Will you come with me to see the spring tomorrow, Cousin Levi?" Luther asked anxiously. "I want you to tell me all about it. Won't you come with me?"

"Of course I will," said Cousin Levi with a smile. "And maybe we can find another spot like that, too. At any rate we can see a good many interesting things. I'm planning to stay over for a few days, so we'll have plenty of time to talk later."

But Luther couldn't wait until later for some of his questions.

"Well, if warm springs can make plants grow all year round," he went on, "why can't we grow flowers and crops by making the air warmer?"

"That could be done," answered his father, "but it would be very expensive. Of course, in California or in the South, the climate is warm all the year round. People there can grow more than one crop a year. But not in New England."

"Don't you remember the letter your brother George wrote?" his mother asked. "He told us of the wonderful things they can grow in California. He said that they can grow squashes that weigh nearly eighty pounds, and that he had seen cabbages that weighed nearly fifty pounds! Their fruits and flowers are much larger than those we grow here, too."

"And it's mostly because of the climate," said Cousin Levi.

"Well, then, someday I want to go to California," Luther declared. "I'll take you with me, Mother. See if I don't," he added as the family laughed.

"But doesn't it take a lot of money to go to California?" asked Alfred.

"Yes," said his mother. "But Luther is still a boy. We don't need to worry about his going so far away, yet."

"I know I'm still a boy," said Luther. "But I'll grow up, and I'll earn some money, and I'll save it. You'll see."

"Good for you, Luther," said Cousin Levi. "But while you are growing up, keep your eyes and ears open and remember all you see and hear."

"I'll remember. I can begin tomorrow when we go to see the spring. Then you can tell me all about it."

"I want to go, too," said Alfred. "Can't I go with you, Cousin Levi? And maybe we'll have time to hunt for nuts."

"I want to go, too," said Emmy, who was

almost asleep by this time. "I want to see the buttercups. Can't I come?"

"Let's wait until tomorrow and then we'll see," said Mrs. Burbank as she picked up the sleepy little sister. "Now it's time for all good children to be in bed."

CHAPTER TWO

• ACCIDENTS CAN HAPPEN •

Luther had forgotten that he would have to go to school when Cousin Levi had said that he was staying over for a few days. But the next morning when Luther got up, he remembered. What a nuisance! Luther was sure that Cousin Levi could teach him all he had to know.

Well, there was no help for it. He would have to hurry home from school. Then he and Cousin Levi could take their walk in the woods.

It was still early when Luther went downstairs. Already his mother was in the kitchen preparing breakfast. Delicious smells of hot bread filled the sunny kitchen. But before he ate he wanted to see if the plants needed watering, and he had to fill the wood boxes.

Each member of the large Burbank family had certain chores to do. Of course David and Eliza-Jane were grown up, so they didn't do chores. David helped his father on the farm and in the brickyard. Eliza taught in the Lancaster Village School.

David and Eliza were not really Luther's own brother and sister. They were the children of his father's former wife. But Luther loved them as much as he did Alfred and Emmy. And he knew that his mother, who was Mr. Burbank's third wife, loved all the children as if they were her own.

By the time Luther was born—he was the thirteenth child—most of the other Burbank children were grown and away from home. The only time Luther saw them was when they came home for Christmas or holidays.

Luther stood for a minute watching his mother hustling around the kitchen. Then he gave her a big hug and started out to the woodshed. He would see to the plants after he brought in the wood.

Luther liked to handle the heavy logs of hickory, maple, oak, and applewood. They smelled so fresh and woodsy, especially when they were burning. He had to make a great many trips. There were many wood boxes to fill, and he could carry only two or three logs at a time. Each time he went into the house, he had a whiff of the good food his mother was preparing.

At last the wood boxes were full. And there was just enough time before breakfast to water the plants.

"Oh, Mother!" he exclaimed as he examined them. "One of the geranium blossoms was leaning on the frosty window and is

frozen. I forgot to put a sheet of paper between it and the glass. I'm so sorry. Should I
cut it off?"

"Yes. It isn't too serious. The plant isn't
hurt," called his mother from the kitchen.

"Just pull the plant a little farther away from the cold windowpane. It will soon blossom again. Perhaps you had better carry the cactus to the window in the other room. It will make room for the other plants. Besides, I think it needs more sun."

"All right, I'll do that." Carefully lifting down the cactus plant, Luther started off for the distant window.

This thornless cactus was his special pride. It was almost the first thing he looked at in the morning and the very last he examined before he went to bed. Perhaps because he was still upset about the frozen geranium, or maybe because he was thinking of the warm spring and the buttercups, Luther tripped on the way. The pot slipped from his hands. Down crashed the precious plant. Pot and plant were broken and scattered over the floor.

Luther was too stunned to move. He stood

gaping at the broken pot and, what was even worse, at the broken cactus plant.

"Mother," he cried. "Oh, Mother, I've broken the cactus plant."

"Now, Luther, stop crying and don't get so upset," said his mother, coming in from the kitchen. "I'm sure the plant isn't ruined. We can repot it, and it will grow again. It won't be quite as big for a while, but time and good care will help. Soon it will be a fine plant again. Now go get another pot and a trowel, and replant it."

Just then Cousin Levi came into the room. "What seems to be the trouble, Luther?" he asked.

"Oh, Cousin Levi, I've broken Mother's beautiful cactus plant, and it will never bloom again."

"Tut-tut, of course it will bloom again," Cousin Levi assured him. "In fact, you can even start a second plant with one of the broken pieces. So stop crying and get me a big pot for the big plant and a small, shallow pot for the new one."

Luther wanted to believe that his cousin knew what he was saying. But he just did not understand how the beautiful plant could survive the rough treatment it had just received.

Cousin Levi mixed some sandy soil with loam and plant food. Then very carefully he cut a broken slab of the thornless cactus and planted it in the soil. Placing the plant on the sunny window, he said, "Don't water it too much. Keep it barely damp. Give it plenty of sun, and before you know it, you will have one more cactus plant. Now let's replant the big one and put it on the windowsill in the other room. Then stop worrying. Someday you'll remember that Cousin Levi and Mother knew what thay were talking about."

In the days that followed Luther did just

what Cousin Levi told him to do. And sure enough, soon he had two cactus plants instead of one. Plants—even a precious cactus—could survive rough treatment.

CHAPTER THREE

. A REAL JOB .

It was Luther's birthday. He was eight years old. He lay with his eyes closed, wishing he didn't have to go school. It would be lots more fun to go for a hike in the woods.

He remembered the walks he and Cousin Levi had taken in the woods just two weeks before. They had walked to the warm spring that Luther had discovered, where tall grasses and green bushes grew in the midst of the ice and snow. They had gone to other warm springs, to the pine woods, and down across the meadow to the brook ponds.

His cousin had told him many interesting

things. He had told him about plants that live in the woods, plants that live on trees, and about water plants that feed on bugs and insects. Luther was anxious to see all these things for himself. Would spring never come?

Just then Alfred, who shared the room with Luther, woke up. Bounding out of bed, Alfred landed on Luther's stomach, shouting, "Happy birthday, Lute. Happy birthday."

This was the signal for a free-for-all, which soon developed into a pillow fight. It was hardly under way before a call to breakfast made the two boys hurry into their clothes.

Shouts of "Happy birthday" greeted Luther again as he and Alfred came down to breakfast. On Luther's plate was a pile of gifts.

Emmy, who couldn't wait for him to get to

her gift, toppled the pile over to find her present. Grabbing it, she handed it to him saying, "I got these all myself. Don't you like them?"

"Let me see them, and I'll tell you," laughed Luther as he hugged his little sister. He opened the package and found an envelope of seeds that she had gathered from the garden.

"How wonderful!" Luther exclaimed. "Will you help me plant them? It won't be long now before we can begin to garden."

"Now look at mine," said Alfred, as he handed his brother a small, heavy parcel. Carefully wrapped in gray-green moss was a bright round stone Alfred had found in the brook. Luther knew it was his brother's prized possession. How nice of him to give it away! he thought.

"Thank you so much, Al. We'll put it on the mantel where everyone can see it and enjoy it. Don't you think that's a good idea?"

Alfred agreed and beamed happily at the suggestion.

Then, turning to the two remaining gifts, Luther found that his mother had knitted him a pair of stockings and a gay green muffler. Green was his favorite color.

He hardly dared open the last present. Because of its shape, he guessed it was a book.

He didn't know which one his father had chosen this time, though any book would please him. Luther opened the package slowly. And then at last he could see the title. It was Henri Fabre's *Book of Insects!*

The book was just what Luther wanted. He remembered the strange stories Cousin Levi had told him about ants and flies and other insects that some plants like to eat. Now he could read about them for himself.

"Now eat your breakfast and stop dreaming," said his mother. "It is getting late, and we all have a lot to do. Besides, you don't want to be late for school. You, Luther, had better eat your porridge so as to be ready for tomorrow's journey."

Luther looked at her questioningly.

"Your father is planning to let you skip school tomorrow," his mother went on. "He is going to let you drive one of the wagonloads of bricks to Lancaster. You can't go unless you have plenty of good food inside you."

"But that is tomorrow," said his father, laughing, "though today's breakfast will help. Would you like to drive the oxen to Lancaster with me? One of the men is ill. I promised to deliver two wagonloads of bricks to the factory, and I need some help. We can start early in the morning, and then we'll have time to rest before we start for home. What do you think?"

"I would love to go with you. I have driven the oxen around the farm lots of times. Besides," Luther hesitated, "I want to see the factory. We'll have time for that, won't we?"

"Let me go, too," begged Alfred. "I can walk that far, and I'm almost as big as Lute."

It was true. Alfred was almost as big as his brother. Though Luther was muscular and wiry, he had not grown fast. His small size often led people to think he was younger than his years.

"No, your turn will come, but not quite yet," Mr. Burbank said kindly. "You and Emmy must help Mother with the chores Luther won't have time to do."

Early next morning Luther was up and dressed. He was too excited to eat the good breakfast his mother had prepared for him. But he knew that she would worry if he didn't eat, so he forced himself to down his porridge.

At last they were off.

"You can lead the way, and I will follow," said Mr. Burbank. "I've given you Buck and Bob. I'm sure you won't have any trouble.

At any rate, you can always wait for me to catch up. Now let's get going." With a wave of the hand to Mrs. Burbank and the two children at the doorway, Mr. Burbank and Luther headed for the barn. The two wagonloads of brick were awaiting their arrival.

Luther felt very proud as he led the team out of the gate. It was the first time he had been given a man's job to do. He hoped Buck and Bob would behave. He didn't want to have to poke them with the goad. Luther knew that oxen were contrary creatures, but he hoped that they would do what he wanted them to do.

They had hardly left the barn behind them, however, when the oxen decided to stop by the wayside. They wanted to eat some of the grass the frost hadn't killed. Luther pulled on the reins. He called out to them as loud as he could. But nothing happened. The oxen refused to move.

Finally, there was nothing to do but to pick up the goad. Luther poked Buck gently at first, then more vigorously, and at last the oxen decided to move slowly on.

It was a long three miles to Lancaster. Luther hadn't remembered that it was so far away. When they finally reached the town and drove into the yard where the men were waiting to receive the bricks, Luther felt he was ready for a long rest.

"Do you want to visit one of the factories after we have lunch?" asked Mr. Burbank as they left the yard. "I'm sure one of the men will be glad to show you around. You will have plenty of time before we start for home."

"Oh, yes," Luther cried, forgetting how tired he was.

Just then a shrill whistle sounded over their heads. Luther was so startled, he fairly jumped.

"Oh, don't mind that," said the foreman, who was walking with them. "It's only the noon whistle to let the men know they can knock off work for lunch. After lunch if you want to see how it works, I'll show it to you."

"Thank you," said Luther. "I would like that. I'll come and find you."

Not only did Luther see how the whistle worked, but he also visited a rug factory and watched the weaving of a rug. He went to one of the grinding mills that was worked by water power, too.

By the time he was ready to start back, his head was so full of new ideas that the road home seemed almost short. Besides, Buck and Bob were less anxious to linger by the roadside. They, too, knew they were headed for home and wanted to get there.

After supper Luther thought over his long and exciting day. He was usually too shy to ask questions or to speak to strangers. But today he had talked freely with the foreman. He had asked endless questions about the machines he had been shown. Now he decided that what others could do, he could do, too, if he tried hard enough. Perhaps I will be able to invent new things, he mused. And with that thought he fell sound asleep.

CHAPTER FOUR

· SUCCESSFUL EXPERIMENT ·

In spite of the chill March wind, Luther knew that another spring had come at last. He and his father had heard the peepers singing at the edge of the pond as they were driving back from Lancaster. And to Luther, the song of the peepers meant that spring had arrived.

It was the day after Luther's trip to Lancaster.

He could hardly wait for school to be over. There were so many things he wanted to do and see. First he wanted to go to the swamp to hunt for pussy willows. They must surely be popping out of their pinkish-red coverings. He would pick some for his mother, who loved the first signs of spring almost as much as he did.

He had hardly stepped into the house that afternoon, when Alfred hailed him.

"Luther, won't you come and look for some willow twigs to make Em and me willow whistles? You made some for us last year, and they were such fun."

"How did you guess that that was what I was going to do?" asked Luther. "I thought of that yesterday when I heard the whistles at the factory. Come on, let's get going."

"I want to come, too," little Em called as she struggled into her coat. "I want to get my own twigs."

"All right, but hurry. It gets dark early. If I am to make the whistles before supper, it's time to go."

The children started off in the direction of

the lower pasture. Luther knew where the finest pussy willow trees grew. They were near the weeping willows from which he would pick the twigs for the whistles. He wanted to stop in the swamp to see if the skunk cabbages and the jack-in-the-pulpits had begun to show. But it was getting late. He would have to do that another time.

Before long the children were back at the farmhouse. Their arms were filled with the soft grayish-pink branches. Emmy wanted to pick off the furry buds. She liked to rub them against her cheek, but Luther refused to let her have more than one branch. He insisted that they were for their mother. She would put them in water, and they could watch the little flowers and leaves develop.

While Emmy carried the pussy willows into the house, Luther and Alfred began to make the whistles. The twigs were fresh and green and moist, the best kind for the job.

"Cut a piece of willow about six inches long," Luther told Alfred, "and I will smooth the end of it. Then I'll cut a notch in it about two inches from the end. Do you think you can tap the twig gently enough to loosen the bark? It has to be stripped off in one piece. Be careful not to break it, or we will have to begin all over again."

Very carefully the two boys worked together. The bark refused to slide off, so Alfred had to soak the twig in water. Finally, the bark slipped off, and Luther cut a groove in the wood at the mouth end. Then the bark was slipped on again. The groove was too small. No sound came out of the whistle. So Alfred had to slip the bark off once more, and Luther cut a deeper and larger groove.

Finally the whistle was finished. Alfred managed to whistle through it loud and long. Much to the boys' delight, Emmy and Mrs. Burbank came running.

This first whistle was for Emmy. The
second one did not take the boys as long to
make. Soon the air resounded with the shrill
noise of the homemade whistles.

Then Luther went to work on a project of
his own. He figured that if steam had had the

power to blow the whistle at the factory, steam could also blow a willow whistle.

The next day he placed a whistle in the spout of an old teakettle. Covering the end of the spout with a small potato, he placed the kettle on the stove. As soon as the kettle began to boil, he removed the potato. The piercing whistle that came out of the spout was so shrill that everyone came running. They were all sure that something terrible had happened.

Mr. Burbank was very angry when he found out what was frightening everyone. Luther was sorry, though secretly pleased at the success of his experiment. He explained the reason for the test and promised his father to be more careful in the future. He had proved that even steam in a kettle has power, which was what he had wanted to find out.

Luther's parents were pleased and proud

of his experiment. They begged him not to try it again, but they were sure that Luther would become a famous inventor when he grew up.

When Luther was a little older, he built a small steam engine that had enough power to move a rowboat through the water. He sold this and added the money to the savings he was storing away for his trip to California. He had not forgotten the promise he had made the night of his discovery of the warm spring. Ever since that night, he was resolved to go to the land that could grow crops and flowers all the year round.

CHAPTER FIVE

· EXPERIMENTS WITH DAISIES ·

It was a still, hot day in June. A gentle breeze stirred the tops of the birches. In the meadows, clovers, daisies, buttercups, and the dainty Queen Anne's lace waved among the tall grasses.

School was over. Luther still had certain chores to do around the farm. But with no school lessons, he had plenty of time for some of the things he had looked forward to doing all spring.

After working in his garden, Luther stopped to rest in the shade of an old apple tree. As he sat looking over the fields that stretched down to the river, he noticed the bees that hummed and buzzed among the flowers. Their busyness fascinated him. He watched a fat bee bury himself in one clover blossom after another. The bee seemed to want to sip the very last drop of sweetness out of every blossom.

Why did he always choose clover blossoms? There were many other fragrant blossoms to dip into. Surely honeysuckle blossoms were sweeter. Instead of looking for honey in a nearby flower, the bee always went from one clover head to another. Luther was curious. He knew this bee was the same one he had first watched, for bees differ from one another just as people do. He must ask Cousin Levi about this.

That night he told his cousin and his cousin's friend, the famous scientist, Dr. Louis Agassiz of Harvard University, what he had seen. Dr. Agassiz and Luther were great friends, so he didn't mind talking or asking questions in front of him.

"Why did the bee take honey only from clovers?" asked Luther. "The honeysuckle blossoms are much more fragrant, and there are many more of them. Besides, it seems to me that it would be easier to get honey from a honeysuckle blossom than from a tiny clover."

"It's true that to you the honeysuckle blossom seems sweeter than the separate blossoms of the clover," said Cousin Levi. "But if a bee begins the day by hunting for nectar, as it is called, in a clover blossom, he will take only that kind of nectar all that day. He never mixes the nectar of different flowers. And because he will not mix the nectar of different flowers, he is a wonderful help to the flowers."

"Did you happen to notice the gold-colored dust on the body of the bee?" asked Dr.

Agassiz. "This dust is called pollen. It is found on the pistil of the flower the bees burrow into.

"The pistil is hollow and resembles a greenish, stemlike tube. Its base is somewhat enlarged. This enlargement is called the ovary. The hollow tubelike stem of the pistil leads down to the ovary, in which the seeds are stored. Because the pistil is sticky, the pollen sticks to the bee's body. It is then carried to the pistil of another flower. In time this pollen makes the seeds from which new plants are grown."

"Oh, so that's the way to get new kinds of plants," said Luther, who had listened to this explanation with great attention. "The pollen of one kind of plant can be put on the pistil of another. How wonderful!"

"That is one way we can improve on nature," said Dr. Agassiz. "Pollen is carried from one flower to another by bees or insects, or wind, or even by water. However, if we want to create a new kind of plant, we take the pollen of one plant and put it on the flower of another. This will produce seeds which may or may not produce a better plant.

"Sometimes we have to experiment with hundreds and even thousands of plants before we get a perfect one. But all imperfect plants must be destroyed, for otherwise they would soon crowd out the good ones. It may take years and years of patient checking, eliminating, and experimenting to get one perfect plant."

Luther thought all this over very carefully. He couldn't get over the idea that new plants could be produced by pollenizing the flowers of different varieties. The subject fascinated him. He looked at every flower he came across and wondered if he could invent new varieties, too.

One day, just as Luther was leaving the

house and heading for the meadow, little Emmy called him. "Luther, where are you going? Can't I go with you?" she asked.

"Well, I suppose so," Luther grudgingly replied. "But you can't take your doll. I'm going down to the brook and coming back by the upper pasture. Are you sure you want to come? It's a long walk."

"Yes I do," said Emmy, who was very positive about her wants. "I'll leave Maria in her carriage on the porch. Then I'll be able to pick some daisies for Mother. Come on. I'm ready."

Sometimes little sisters are a nuisance, thought Luther, who wanted to go off by himself. But he loved little Emmy and hated to refuse her. So, taking her warm little hand in his, he started off.

"Let's go through the big meadow, Lute," said Emmy. "I want to pick some daisies." Once Emmy got an idea into her head, she clung to it.

"All right, but you mustn't pick flowers until we get back," said Luther. "They'll fade, and that would be too bad. We can have fun looking at them, and you can see where the biggest ones are. Then, on our way back, you can pick them. I'll help you."

As the children crossed the meadow, Luther, whose eyes were busily examining the many wild flowers, suddenly exclaimed, "Oh, Emmy, wait. There is the most beautiful daisy I ever saw. It is almost perfect. Look at the petals. They are large and shining white. And the center is golden yellow!

"I'm going to plant it in my garden. Then I'll plant another near it and pollenize them. When they begin to make seeds, I'll save them. Next year, maybe, if I take good care of the plants, I'll have even bigger flowers. But I mustn't uproot them now. They might wither. What shall I do?"

"Tie a piece of string around the big one,

and then you'll find it," suggested Emmy.

"I haven't any string," said Luther. "Besides, it wouldn't show up in the tall grass. I'll just have to tear off a piece of my blue shirt."

"Mother won't like it, Lute," said Emmy. "And what does pollen, or whatever you said, mean?"

"Never mind that now," answered Luther. "Mother will understand about the shirt. I must find that plant again. Come on. Let's go to the brook."

It was shady under the big pines, and the water in the slow-moving brook was tempting.

"I want to put my feet in the water, Luther," coaxed Emmy. "Help me."

"All right, but don't fall in. Here, you'd better sit on this rock and dangle your feet in the water. I want to look around a bit."

Wading was no problem, for the children

were barefoot. They wore stockings only on Sunday. Since Mrs. Burbank knitted all their stockings, and the family was a large one, stockings were saved for the Sabbath.

Luther noticed that the ferns and the moss along the stream were still lush and green. However, farther down, the ground in which the cattails grew was barely swampy. The water seemed almost to have disappeared. Then he remembered what his cousin had told him the day they had hunted for the warm spring.

They had been talking about how plants get their food. Cousin Levi had said that some plants, called parasites, live on other plants and take their food directly from them. As for water, he had said that many of them take it out of the ground with their roots. Some of the water makes food, while some of it goes off into the air. Some plants need more water than others.

Then Cousin Levi had added, "Remember the cattails you like to cut in summer to put in the house? Your stream is full of them. But in July, because they drink so much, there will be almost no water where they grow."

Luther had looked at the rushing stream and had hardly believed that cattails could drink as much as Cousin Levi had said. But now he saw for himself that it was so. The ways of plants were certainly interesting. He would tell his cousin what he had seen.

But he had better get back to Emmy. By this time she would no doubt be soaking wet. He had left her splashing her feet up and down in the water.

"My, oh my, you are wet!" he exclaimed, as he came up to her. "Let's get in the sun. Maybe you can dry off while you pick your flowers."

For a while nothing was said. Luther was busy uprooting his daisy plants, and Emmy ran here and there gathering her bouquet.

"Look, Mother," Emmy called as they reached the farmhouse. "I picked a bunch of all kinds of flowers for you. Do you like them?"

"They are lovely," said Mrs. Burbank. "But what is Luther doing?"

"Oh, he found a daisy plant he wanted for his garden." Emmy looked quite disgusted. "I don't see why he had to get it when there are so many in the meadow."

"But Mother," Luther explained, as he proudly showed her two of the daisies, "this one is an exceptionally fine plant, and I took this other one because I want to try an experiment. Remember what Dr. Agassiz said about pollenizing plants? Maybe I can get some seeds from them and I can grow a whole garden of beautiful big white daisies."

"That would be wonderful," said his mother, smiling. "But I don't think your

father will like this. You know he dislikes daisies and thinks they are bad for cattle."

"I know, but I won't let them spread out of my garden, I promise," said Luther earnestly.

"Well, let's wait and see what happens,"

said his mother. She knew how much this experiment meant to Luther. And she thought that a bed of beautiful big white daisies would be worth seeing.

Though Mr. Burbank grumbled and considered this daisy-plant business a waste of time, he didn't forbid it. He knew Luther would keep his promise not to let the plants spread beyond his garden.

Luther carefully took the pollen of each daisy plant and transferred it to the flower of the other one. He hoped the seeds from these would produce beautiful flowers.

Alas, the experiment was disappointing. A great many plants did come up from the seeds he planted, but they were not beautiful. They were not the big white-petaled flowers he had hoped for. Instead, they were thin-petaled, small, straggly flowers. Mrs. Burbank was afraid Luther would be disappointed.

"Never mind," said Luther, examining the poor specimens. "I will have to try again. Perhaps if I get better plants to begin with, I'll have better luck. Dr. Agassiz said it might take hundreds and even thousands of plants before a perfect one can be produced. He said I must always burn all the poor plants, which means all of them this time. I'll just have to keep on trying. Someday I'll really produce the finest white daisy anyone has ever seen. Wait and see if I don't."

CHAPTER SIX

· A PRACTICAL INVENTION ·

The bright summer days sped by all too quickly. Luther hated to think that soon he would have to go back to school. There was so much he wanted to do. The days weren't long enough.

Luther had had long talks and walks with his Cousin Levi. His cousin had shown him how a small twig could be grafted onto the branch of a larger tree. "You must work carefully," said Cousin Levi. "Fruit trees grow slowly, so this is one way of getting different kinds of fruit quickly. If you have patience, you will see for yourself what will happen."

"Do you mean that all kinds of apples can be grown on one tree?" Luther asked. "Can a twig of a red apple tree, of a yellow apple, and of a green apple be grafted on the same tree? Will they all grow?"

"Not only can you make all kinds of apples grow on one tree, but by grafting pear twigs on an apple tree, pears can be made to grow on it, too. Or," Cousin Levi added smiling, "apples can be grown on pear trees."

How wonderful! Luther could hardly wait to experiment. Must he wait until he was grown up? Whenever he looked at an apple tree, he pictured it covered with fruit of every variety. His mind was filled with all sorts of plans.

Today he and Alfred had been playing ball in the orchard. They were hot and were resting in the shade, each munching a red, juicy apple.

"Why are the nicest apples always where

I can't reach them?" grumbled Alfred.

"I don't know, Al," answered Luther. "But someday, do you know what I am going to do? I'm going to invent a small tree that any child can reach."

"Ho! You know perfectly well you can't invent a tree. Only God can make a tree grow," laughed Alfred.

"Well, I can't exactly invent a tree," answered Luther, "but when I get to California, I'll find a small tree just the right size. Then I'll graft some apple twigs on it. And then do you know what I'll do? I'll have red apples and yellow apples and green cooking apples all on the same tree.

"Cousin Levi told me I could even grow pears on an apple tree. He showed me how to graft the twigs. So, when you want a certain apple or pear you won't have to walk all through the orchard to find it. Won't that be fine?"

"Oh, Lute, you're crazy," laughed Alfred. "You can't make that kind of tree. You know you can't."

"Just wait and see. When I'm grown up and live in California, I'll do anything I want to do. Then I'll say, 'Didn't I tell you I would?' "

But Luther's vacation days were not all spent in playing. Mr. Burbank expected each one of his children to help on the farm. Luther weeded the vegetable gardens and helped David and the men bring in the hay. He drove the oxen into Lancaster with loads of bricks for the factories or with lumber for the paper mills. All this didn't leave much free time to work at some of his own projects.

Though Luther liked best to wander in the fields and woods studying the flowers, trees, and wild life, he liked making things almost as much. He made statuary and bowls from the clay in the brickyard. He made water wheels and windmills. Whatever he did had a practical value. Because of his mechanical ability his father was sure that he would become a mechanic.

However, Mrs. Burbank was not quite so sure of this. She knew how much Luther enjoyed working and experimenting with plants.

But vacation days don't last forever, and soon Luther was back at school. Though not brilliant in his studies, his eagerness to learn and his curiosity about the world around him made him stand out among the students at the Academy. His teachers enjoyed teaching a boy who wanted to learn.

Although he attended school six days a week, every other Saturday afternoon was free. Luther always looked forward to this time. It was on such an afternoon that, having changed into his old clothes, he began his work on a dam. He wanted to build it in

the brook that ran in the big meadow. He was hard at work when his father appeared on the bank above him.

"What do you think you are doing, Luther,

wasting your time playing in the brook?" he asked. "You can't dam up this brook. It will overflow when the rains come and will cover the fields."

"I know," said Luther. "That's why I am building the dam right here. Ice will cover the meadow, and we'll have a grand skating pond." Then seeing his father's frown, he added, "Besides, the water that covers these lowland pastures will make a bigger swamp next summer. That will give you more land on which to grow cranberries. Next autumn you will have larger cranberry bogs."

"Hm! Maybe that's a good idea," said Mr. Burbank, turning away. Luther's ideas were often worth listening to.

Things worked out exactly as Luther planned. It took many Saturday afternoons of hard work to build the dam. But by the time winter came, the meadows were covered with a thick layer of ice. Luther's skating pond idea had succeeded.

Though Luther was thin and frail, he was very quick. He soon became the expert skater of the neighborhood. Every afternoon the boys and girls from the neighboring farms would gather at the Burbank pond. The happy shouts and calls of the youngsters at play echoed in the winter twilight. Luther's invention was a success.

CHAPTER SEVEN

· LUTHER, MARKET GARDENER ·

Luther was growing up. He was in his teens. He could no longer spend all summer on the farm. Because he showed unusual mechanical ability, his father decided to put him to work in the woodworking department of a manufacturing company at Worcester.

His first duty was to make plow-rounds for which he received fifty cents a day. As he paid fifty cents a day for board and only worked six days a week, this arrangement did not suit him. After all, he wanted to eat on the seventh day, too.

Luther soon persuaded his uncle, the superintendent, to pay him by the piece instead of by the day. This plan worked out well for Luther because he had invented a new kind of lathe. With this lathe he could turn out work much faster. Now he could earn as much as sixteen dollars a day, and he wanted money. He never forgot that someday he would go to California.

Soon Luther was producing more plow-rounds than the factory could dispose of, and his uncle could not afford to pay him for as many as he could make. Luther's uncle suggested that Luther try inventing other things instead. So Luther went home to think this over.

Instead of inventing, however, he decided to study art. But he soon discovered that this wasn't what he really wanted to do either.

Then, during an illness brought on by over-exertion in the hot sun, he became interested in medicine. He asked many questions of the doctor who visited him every day. Perhaps this was what he was looking for. He would become a doctor!

Luther studied medicine for a year. He might have gone on with it if his father had not died. But after his father's death, he knew that he had to give up his studies and devote all his time to earning money.

Luther was now twenty-one. His health had never been too good. The dust from the work in the lumber factory had affected it. It seemed to him as he thought about what he should do that working outdoors would be just what he needed. So he decided to grow fruits and vegetables for market.

It seemed as if all his life Luther had been trained in the work that gardeners and fruit-growers had to do. And he had always been interested in plants of all kinds. But it was not until now, when he was twenty-one, that he began to devote all his time and energy to becoming a practical market gardener and seed raiser.

Luther bought seventeen acres of fine land not far from Lancaster. There was an old house on the place, and here he settled down as a market gardener. He soon found that in spite of his background he had much to learn. He was competing against experienced gardeners who had many steady customers.

Luther decided that the only way he could compete with the well-established market gardeners was to raise better vegetables and to get them to market earlier than any of the others.

Cousin Levi's oft-repeated "Use your eyes and head" stood him in good stead. To get better vegetables, he needed to produce better plants. To produce plants that were better than those that were generally accepted, he would have to experiment and develop new varieties. He must also think of ways to make these varieties produce their vegetables earlier.

The thought of getting superfine vegetables to market ahead of anyone else was exciting and challenging to Luther. As he began to plan and experiment with plants, he remembered the beautiful green grass and shrubs he had found in the woods that winter's day. He remembered the warm spring that had made this growth possible.

He found that by sprouting sweet corn in a hot bed, he could set the young plants out in the fields long before anyone else. This meant that he was able to have corn for sale ahead of his competitors. In this way he obtained higher prices for his early corn and made many new customers.

But Luther wasn't content with plants that were earlier and just a little better. He knew that he should be able to create much better ones.

About this time he read Darwin's *Animals and Plants Under Cultivation*. This confirmed his old idea that he could "invent" new plants, new seeds, and new roots. This was what he had always wanted to do. Just as soon as he had enough money, he decided, he would go to California and really get started. There he could do more easily all of the things he wanted to do.

Like most market gardeners, Luther raised quantities of potatoes. They were a small, red variety, called Early Rose. This potato didn't keep very well. So Luther had tried over and over again by cross-pollenizing the blossoms to produce seed. From seed, he hoped to produce a larger and more tasty potato. But for a long time he had little success.

Then, one day while Luther was examining each potato vine for potato bugs, he came to a sudden stop. There, on a vine, grew a small green ball, a seed pod full of potato seeds.

Seed balls of this kind are rare, for potatoes are grown most often by cutting tubers and planting them.

Luther was excited. Who knows what kind of potatoes might be grown from the seeds! Having no cloth or any way in which to mark the vine, he did as he had done with the daisy plant years before. He tore off a piece of his shirttail and tied this on the vine. He knew he would have to wait many weeks for the pod to ripen, but the seeds were worth waiting for.

Hurrying home, he rushed into the house, calling, "Mother, Mother, what do you think I've found? A seed ball on my Early Rose potato vine!"

"But Luther, you know very well that potatoes aren't grown from seeds. And look, you've torn your shirt again," she said, pointing to the ragged shirttail.

"I'm sorry, Mother, but I had to mark that

plant. I'll watch that seed pod, and when it is ripe I'll plant the seeds. Who knows what kind of potatoes I'll get?"

"Remember what happened to your daisy seeds, Luther," cautioned his mother.

But nothing could discourage Luther. Every day he watched the seed ball getting bigger and riper. And while he waited for it to ripen, he dreamed of how he would sell the perfect potato that would grow from one of the seeds. From the money he would get, he would go to California.

Alas, one morning as he ran hopefully toward the vine, his heart almost stopped beating. The seed ball had disappeared. It couldn't be lost! Carefully, row by row, vine by vine, he searched the ground. All day he hunted. Then, just as he was about to give up, he found the precious seed ball.

There were only twenty-three seeds in it, but they were ripe. The seeds were so tiny that Luther could hardly believe they would produce any kind of potato. He could hardly wait to see what would grow from them. But he would have to wait until spring before he could even put them in the ground.

Spring and mild weather finally came. Luther planted the seeds very carefully in a specially prepared plot. In time vines appeared, and at last the day came when he could dig the potatoes.

He had given each seed hill the same attention. To his surprise each seed produced a different type of tuber. Hill by hill, he examined the potatoes. In each hill he hoped to find the potato he was looking for. But the potatoes were small and knobby.

Finally, when he had almost reached the last hill, one cluster seemed larger as he dug down. And when he got the potatoes out, he found that they were indeed larger. They were wonderfully big, well-shaped tubers.

They were such beautifully colored, juicy potatoes Luther could hardly keep from shouting aloud. He knew he had found a brand-new potato that people everywhere would like.

CHAPTER EIGHT

· DOING THE IMPOSSIBLE ·

The following year Luther sold the potato to a practical gardener for one hundred and fifty dollars. The purchaser let him keep ten potatoes, and gave him permission to introduce the new variety elsewhere.

Now Luther could go to California. His dream of migrating to a place where the climate would help him grow fine plants was coming true.

When he had sold his farm and all its equipment, he was ready to start out. He was sorry to say good-by to his mother. California seemed far away. It would take him at least nine days to reach the Pacific coast. But he knew that his decision to go to a warmer climate was a wise one. Though he was sad to be leaving home, it was with a feeling of excitement that he set out. The year was 1875.

Luther was twenty-six years old. He was a small, wiry, and active young man, full of curiosity and enthusiasm. All his life he had been interested in and curious about plants, and for over ten years he had worked with them. He had done a lot of reading, and his Cousin Levi and Dr. Agassiz had given him a good grounding in natural science. He knew exactly what he wanted to do.

He knew he wanted to produce more beautiful and finer flowers, new and better-flavored fruits and vegetables, and sturdier and heavier-bearing grains. It was an ambitious program.

Luther had pored over maps and bulletins put out by the Union Pacific Railroad. So he knew just about where he wanted to settle. He chose Santa Rosa as most suitable to his plans. In one of his first letters home after his arrival he wrote, "I firmly believe, from what I have seen, that it is the *chosen* spot of *all this earth* as far as *Nature* is concerned." He knew he had chosen well.

His two brothers, who were already living in California, though not in the same town, were anxious to help him get established. But Luther didn't want to trouble them. He knew they had enough problems of their own. Besides, he also knew that they didn't approve of his plans, so he felt that it was better not to bother them.

However, one of them did help him build an 8-by-10 shanty. After Luther had purchased crockery, bedding, etc., he was almost ready to settle down and begin work. But first he spent a week or two roaming about the hillsides, examining the curious plants and

wild flowers he had never seen before. He longed to experiment with some of them.

Luther was a good carpenter, so for a while he worked at that trade. Such work was not always to be had, and there were many days when he wondered if he would have enough money for food. But Luther never grew discouraged. He knew what he wanted to do, and he intended to do it.

After a while he got a job helping in a nursery. He saved every cent he could. And finally he was able to rent a few acres of land for himself. After that, all his free time was spent in developing a nursery of his own. Only after he had a good business could he spend time experimenting.

He planted his ten potatoes, and the sale from this crop helped a little. Californians were used to a red potato, not a white one. So it took some time before this Burbank potato, as it was named, became generally accepted. When this fine white potato did become known, however, it became the best-selling potato on the Pacific coast.

But the potato business was not enough. Luther wanted to raise other things and develop other plants, too. It took a long time for him to build up his business. It took hard work and perseverance, but finally he began to see success.

At first the greater part of his business consisted of raising the fruits and vegetables the Santa Rosans knew and used. Luther remembered his experience with the early corn and fine crops he had grown in the East. He applied the same ideas now, and soon he was producing crops that were better and ripened earlier than the crops of other gardeners.

In about five years Luther Burbank's nursery was well known and firmly established. His reputation for reliability and for the quality of his stock was spreading. As soon as his business was commercially successful, he decided that it was time to experiment with the various plants in his nursery.

As soon as he could afford it, he bought four acres of land in Santa Rosa and established a garden in which to carry out his experiments. Later he bought eighteen more acres at Sebastopol, about seven miles outside of Santa Rosa. Here the climate and local conditions were different from those of his garden at Santa Rosa. But he felt that it was an even better location.

No one believed in the idea that new and useful plants could be created, or that old plants might be grown in new ways. But Luther refused to listen to these doubters. To him there was no such word as "impossible." He believed that if you truly wanted to do a thing, you would find a way to do it. It might take a long time and you might need lots of patience, but it could be done.

It was in March of 1881 that Luther had an unexpected opportunity to prove that he could do what seemed "impossible" to others. A certain rich banker and merchant, a Mr. Dutton came to see him. Mr. Dutton had taken a sudden interest in prune growing and was anxious to establish a large orchard as quickly as possible. Could Mr. Burbank furnish 20,000 prune trees that would be ready to set out in the fall of the year?

Everyone seemed to think this was impossible, but not Luther. He thought the matter over very carefully and decided it could be done. He knew that almond trees, which are closely related to prune trees, grow rapidly. If Mr. Dutton would furnish the money for almond seeds and for the help he would need, Luther agreed to supply the 20,000 prune trees on time.

He knew that with proper care he could get almond seeds to grow quickly. Then he would transplant the seedling trees into rows. He planted his seeds carefully, and in fourteen days the seedling trees were ready to transplant. He removed them carefully and planted them in rows four feet apart.

By the end of June the buds on his prune trees in his own orchard were ready for grafting. Now he was ready to go ahead with his plan. He hired a large force of men to graft the French prune buds on the almond stalks.

In the days that followed, Luther watched the trees with great care. But he did not worry about the success of his plan. He knew that it would work.

The first of December 19,500 prune trees were delivered to Mr. Dutton. The rest were furnished in the spring of the following year. Mr. Dutton was delighted and amazed. Everyone had told him that it was absolutely impossible to produce 20,000 prune trees in so short a time. Luther had done the impossible!

This success proved of great importance to Luther, for it not only brought him much-needed money, but it helped greatly to advertise his work.

Then, too, prunes were beginning to prove a profitable crop, and the demand for stock from the Burbank Nursery was great. Luther's reputation for reliability was established more firmly than ever.

The success of Luther's work with the prune trees also encouraged him to try other "impossible" tasks. And most of them were successful, because he knew what he was doing, and he took pains to do it right.

CHAPTER NINE

· LUTHER, NATURE'S HELPER ·

Though we think of California as a fruit-growing state, when Luther first came to Santa Rosa he found that it was chiefly a wheat-growing country. It was only when the wheat crops began to fail that farmers turned to the growing of fruit. But fruit-growing was not so profitable for the farmers as it ought to have been.

Luther realized that the different fruits raised in California at that time were the same as those grown in the East. They were not especially fitted for the climate of the Pacific coast. So he decided to develop orchard fruits—plums, prunes, and peaches—that, in time, would be the basis of an important fruit industry for California.

He wanted to produce trees that would be hardy, that would grow in spite of unfavorable conditions, and that would produce steadily and in great quantities. And he wanted to produce fruit that could withstand long-distance shipment.

Fortunately for Luther, transportation by railroad, and modern packing methods soon made the sending of fresh fruit for long distances possible. Now that his nursery business was prospering, he had time and money with which to carry on experiments more widely. His success in furnishing the 20,000 prune trees on time had added to his reputation.

One day, while browsing in a library in San Francisco, he came across a description of a "blood-red plum" found in Japan. So mouth-watering was the description of this plum, that Luther immediately ordered a dozen seedlings sent him. These were the foundation of his plum experiments.

So well did Luther succeed that in less than four years he was able to market a large, red, juicy, firm plum with a delicious flavor. Because the original seedlings had come from Japan, it was named the Satsuma.

But Luther was not satisfied with this first success. His plums were better than any that had ever been produced, but he felt that still better plums were possible. He collected more plum stocks and continued to experiment. He made test after test and experiment after experiment for many years. He worked hard and patiently, spending much time and money on the growing of thousands of specimens. From these he hoped to get a few perfect specimens.

Although he found only thirty or forty

perfect specimens from the thousands he had planted, he continued his experiments. Finally, by 1893, he had created more than twelve new varieties of plums and prunes, all better than any of the old ones had been.

But still Luther was not finished. As he continued to experiment, he chose plants from all over the world. He combined into a single new variety the bright color and delicious fragrance of the Chinese plum, the large size and hardness of the Japanese plum, the fine flavor of the wild American plum, and the sweetness of the small European plum. Today hundreds of carloads of these plums are shipped all over America every season.

Luther also wanted to produce a stoneless plum. So he decided to experiment with the stoneless French plum. It took a long time and much experimenting before he finally succeeded in producing a large stoneless plum with the delicious quality he wanted.

Later he crossed the plum with the apricot and created the plumcot. This new species had all the hardness of the plum, but the fragrance and flavor of the apricot.

When Luther had created about twenty new varieties of plum, he published a catalog with a full description of each new fruit. This was sent to nurserymen all over the world who bought stock from him. In turn, these nurserymen grew stock from these plants and sold them to fruitgrowers. Luther's business and reputation increased, and his work became known all over the world.

Many of Luther's ideas of plant breeding were not new. They had been used by horticulturists for years. Luther only improved on old ways of doing things. His unusually keen vision, a fine sense of color, and a well-developed sense of smell and taste were of especial help in weeding out poorer speci-

mens and keeping the finer plants.

His eye responded quickly to details.
Luther was able to select the right specimen
with an amazing correctness. So wonderful
was his skill in choosing the finest specimen
with which to experiment that men began to
think of him as having special powers of

magic. He was often called the "Wizard of Santa Rosa."

But Luther didn't think of himself as having special powers. He always claimed that it was only by repeating experiment after experiment that he got to know a good specimen from a poor one. He maintained that he was just a "plant experimenter" anxious to produce fine seeds and plants. He was only helping nature do what she could not do by herself.

Luther's ideas of how to produce new and improved varieties of plants were quite simple. He believed in choosing plants that showed exceptional qualities and planting their seeds. This process eventually produced better, stronger plants. He also believed that stronger and more unusual varieties could be obtained by cross-pollenizing these strong plants.

Followed by his helper, Luther would stride along a row of seedlings in which there might be thousands of foot-high trees. He would glance at them and with a slight gesture indicate those which should be saved. To these the helper would attach a strip of cloth. Luther would examine these carefully later and perhaps save fifty or a hundred of them for future use when doing other experiments.

The rest of the plants were dug up and burned. Luther remembered Dr. Agassiz' advice: "Destroy all but perfect specimens." Though this meant burning thousands of seedlings, he never hesitated to do so.

So keen was his eyesight that the examination of ten thousand little trees took but half an hour. The few trees that survived the test were then carefully treasured and given every attention.

Luther believed that it was important to study the habits and growth of the plants he wanted to improve. He spent much time in studying the background of the plants he wanted to use in his experiments.

He also believed that young plants, like young children, should receive special care and attention if they are to grow strong. He believed that everything depends upon the treatment the seedling receives the first days or weeks of its life. It needs the right soil, the right amount of moisture and sunlight, and protection from the wind. He was convinced that the future life of the plant depended largely on its early treatment.

These methods Luther used not only on plums and prunes but on other fruits as well. His experiments with berries and orchard fruits were wonderfully successful.

He produced an ever-bearing strawberry that was the most delicious yet grown. He created many varieties of raspberries, blueberries, and blackberries.

Luther resented the thorns that attacked him whenever he picked blackberries, so he set out to find a vine that would be thornless. The first ones he managed to "invent" had only a few thorns, and these thorns were without points. But this did not satisfy him, for the berries did not have much taste.

For almost thirty years he worked with

the blackberry vine, pollenizing and cross-pollenizing vine after vine. Finally he succeeded. He produced a delicious, juicy blackberry that grew on a thornless vine.

At the same time, Luther was also experimenting with peaches, apples, cherries, and other fruit trees. He produced peach trees that could withstand freezing weather, and trees that had freestone peaches that were not only big and beautiful but had a delicious taste and fragrance.

In working with apples, instead of planting seedlings in rows, he used one big tree on which he grafted many varieties. As a little boy he had promised his brother Alfred that he would "invent" a small apple tree that would bear several kinds of apples on the one tree. His experiments were a carrying out of that childhood dream.

On one tree he had as many as 526 varieties of apples at one time. Working in this way he

saved time and energy which would ordinarily be spent going up and down the various rows. By climbing a ladder he could examine each twig and watch its development.

Though Luther only introduced two new varieties of apples, he improved the growth and development of many varieties that were already known.

When he experimented with cherry trees, he used the same method he had used with apples. At times one cherry tree had as many as 500 different varieties. By careful hybridization and selection he created the Burbank cherry, which was an early-ripening, large, delicious-flavored cherry. Its hardiness also assured safe shipment.

Whenever Luther undertook a new project, he remembered his Cousin Levi's advice: "It is useless to grow new plants unless they are an improvement on the old." But Luther felt that all plants could be improved. Vegetables as well as fruits could be improved by increased size and better flavor. As he worked he also developed new varieties. By selective breeding he managed to produce many new types of peas, beans, Spanish onions, corn, and many other garden vegetables.

It took years of time and endless patience and hard work to accomplish all that Luther did, but nothing was too difficult for him to attempt.

CHAPTER TEN

• PLANT EXPERIMENTER •

In time Luther was no longer pressed for money or for time. His business was a success. Men from all over the world bought from his nursery. Now he could give some attention to the growing and improvement of flowers. This was something he had always wanted to do.

If he had followed his own wishes, he would have spent all of his time developing flowers. But knowing that he could never make a living with just these, he had first turned his attention to developing fruits and vegetables that could be sold to other nurserymen.

As far back as he could remember, Luther had always loved flowers. He had looked forward to the time when he could experiment with them, creating new and more beautiful varieties.

In the late spring the California hills and valleys were covered with hundreds of wild flowers of all kinds and colors. Among them were the bright orange-gold poppies. When Luther first saw the hillsides covered with millions of these lovely flowers, he thought it was the most beautiful sight he had ever seen. He liked to believe that the early explorers entering San Francisco Bay had named it "The Golden Gate" because of the brilliant poppies on the hills opposite the entrance to the harbor.

He never tired of admiring and examining them. He found that they varied in size, color, and even in shape, according to where they grew. Those that grew along the seacoast were larger than those in the inland valleys. Those that grew in the valley, however, were darker in color, and according to their location, varied in height and manner of growth.

He discovered that some showed a thin line of red running up the center of the petal. Carefully keeping the seeds of these plants, he planted them. After cross-pollenizing them for several generations, he was able to produce large poppies with crimson petals. By selection and repetition over a long period of years, he succeeded in producing poppies ranging in color from white to deepest red.

As a child, Luther had tried to grow a large white daisy with a big golden center from plants he had found in the field. This first attempt had not been successful. Now, however, he was ready to try again. He still wished to produce "the most beautiful daisy in the world."

He tried all kinds of seeds and plants. Finally, by always eliminating the poorer specimens, he succeeded in getting a daisy that was much larger and more beautiful than the original he had planted. But it was not so large or so white as the one he was hunting for.

So he decided to take a Japanese daisy that had a small but dazzling white flower and cross it with the large hybrid blossom he had already developed. Then he crossed this one with a large Michaelmas daisy from England. And last of all he crossed these with the sturdy New England daisy that flowers profusely.

He worked carefully at all times. Just as he had tried to cross-pollenize the one kind of daisy plant in his boyhood garden, he now cross-pollenized the many kinds of daisies. Instead of working with only a few plants, he now pollenized many flowers of each variety.

He cleaned the seeds from these plants and planted them in shallow boxes called flats. Each tiny seedling was examined as it appeared and the undesirable ones were destroyed. The perfect specimens were then transplanted in a test bed.

Day by day he continued to examine these plants, and one by one the weak ones were eliminated. As the strong ones matured, they were cross-pollenized and the seeds kept and again planted. Then, only the best of these were kept.

In time, by always selecting only the best specimens and eliminating the poor ones, he succeeded in producing what everyone declared was "the most beautiful daisy in all the world." He named it the "Shasta daisy" for the nearby mountain he loved so much.

The Shasta daisy will grow almost anywhere. It requires little care and produces many large, golden-hearted, wax-white blossoms. Many other varieties of this daisy have been developed since the first one was produced.

For many years Luther also experimented with lilies. He wanted them not only to be hardy, healthy, and to multiply quickly, but also to be fragrant and beautiful, and to produce many flowers. The calla lily, which grows so well in the California climate, was beautiful, but it was without fragrance. This was a challenge that tempted him. He began to experiment with it.

He had been working with the lily for a long time when one day as he was inspecting a field of the flowers, he suddenly realized that one, among the thousands of flowers in the field, had an all-pervading perfume. He had succeeded in developing a perfumed calla lily, but now he had to locate the fragrant one.

It was late and it would soon be dark. Luther couldn't afford to wait until morning. The blossom might fade; almost anything might happen. So crawling slowly along on hands and knees, he went from row to row until he found the blossom with the marvelous perfume. The fragrance of this lily became world famous.

In the years that followed, Luther produced so many varieties of lilies that he did not exaggerate when he said, "Search this earth all over, climb every mountain . . . go anywhere and everywhere, and as many varieties of charming lilies cannot be found, as I have produced."

Thanks to Luther Burbank's tireless patience and endless experiments, today we can enjoy all kinds of new varieties of the flowers. There are not only different kinds, but they are larger, more fragrant, and are sturdier and grow more abundantly than the flowers they originally came from. It would be difficult to list all the flowers Luther worked with. There are endless varieties of roses, dahlias, galdioli, and many of the little annuals which we now take for granted.

But Luther did not confine his efforts to developing only the more showy plants. A project that took him more than sixteen years to perfect was the creation of the spineless cactus. He claimed that he learned more from the experiments with cacti than from any other work he attempted. It showed him how really great were the possibilities that exist in plant breeding.

The huge cacti of the deserts of the Southwest, with their sharp spines, fascinated him. He remembered the spineless cactus plant he had loved and cared for as a boy on the farm. Could he produce a spineless cactus that would grow and flourish on arid ground?

Ranchmen told him that when rain was scarce and crops failed, they would burn off the spines of the cactus plants without hurting the plants and would feed these plants to their cattle. The cacti contained ninety-eight per cent water and some nourishment. The cattle seemed to relish them as food. But burning off the spines was a long and tedious job which ranchmen hated to undertake.

Luther knew that because of their long spines cacti were almost impossible to handle.

Plants without spines, however, could provide fodder for cattle the year round.

So Luther went to work. To his surprise he found that there were a thousand varieties of cactus plants. The first thing to do was to

get as many varieties as possible. He obtained over six hundred from all over the world. These were shipped to him at Santa Rosa at a cost of thousands of dollars. He also hired a crew of men to help him.

Finally he was ready to start his experiments. Slabs of the cacti he had bought were planted, as many as 6,000 a day. At first Luther wore gloves to handle them, for the spines were sharp and dangerous. But he found that the gloves slowed the work. So in spite of the fact that millions of cactus needles pierced the skin of his face and hands, he worked without the gloves.

Not only were the thorns of tremendous size, but the plants, too, grew big and tall. It was no easy matter to handle the heavy slabs.

As the plants blossomed, Luther crossed the pollen of one with another by rubbing the stamen of one on the pistil of the other. This had to be done just as soon as the flower began to bloom, before the bees had a chance to get at them. As soon as the fruit appeared and ripened, Luther cut it open and collected the seeds.

As he worked, Luther kept careful records

of each process so that he knew exactly what each plant was doing. The seeds were carefully planted. Those that did not measure up to what was expected were destroyed. It was most important to pick the right varieties. Luther wanted to produce plants that not only would have no spines, but that would also have great food value and would grow quickly and without much care.

After years of careful experimentation, he developed a spineless cactus with all the desired qualities. This plant not only contained ninety per cent water, but it also had sugar and mineral elements of value to cattle. And what was also important, one acre could produce from 150 to 300 tons of fodder.

In addition to its use as fodder for cattle, the fruit of the cactus is delicious and nutritious. Though some cactus pears are not entirely without spines, they are easy to handle. Before long the fruit became popular.

Luther had solved the cattlemen's fodder problem in this country. And because cacti slabs of these plants were sold all over the world, cattlemen in far countries grew rich with the crop, too. They were willing to pay big prices for sample plants.

CHAPTER ELEVEN

· THE WIZARD OF SANTA ROSA ·

With the income from the sale of the spineless cactus, Luther was able to build a fine
new house. It was across the road from a
small house he had been living in for many
years.

Luther's home life was a happy one. He
had a fine devoted wife who shared his interest and enthusiasm. Her niece, Betty Jane,
lived with them. Luther used to romp and
play with Betty Jane until Mrs. Burbank
could hardly stand the noise. The "Big Chief"
and Betty Jane would roar, dance, and roll
on the floor. As Mrs. Burbank said, they were

· 117 ·

much worse than a houseful of growing boys.

The fourth member of the Burbank household was Luther's mother. As a boy, planning the work he hoped to accomplish in the longed-for California life, his mother had always been a part of the picture. So when business prospered, his mother came to share Luther Burbank's home. This was the realization of one more of his childhood dreams.

It wasn't always easy for his mother to enter into Luther's plans. So when the time came to move into the new home he had built, she refused. She was used to the little house and liked it better. The fact that the new house was just across the road didn't make any difference. She remained set in her ways, and Luther had a hard time getting her to agree to the change. However, Luther's sense of fun saved the day.

"Look, Mother," he said. "How would you like to travel? By taxi? By tally-ho? Or

would you prefer to go by piggy back?"

Mrs. Burbank smiled. Near by stood a wheelbarrow. She pointed to it. Picking her up in his arms, Luther placed her in the wheelbarrow and in the midst of laughter, wheeled her across the road to the new home.

Luther Burbank was a gentle, quiet man, who was loved and admired by thousands who never saw him. His mail and correspondence were enormous. People all over the world —people who had never known or met him— wrote to him for advice and information. And he was never too busy to help them.

Friends, strangers, the great, and the not-so-great visited him, especially after he moved to his new home. They walked through his gardens and greenhouses, admiring, questioning, and learning. Some came just to see the "great magician"; some to pay the homage they knew he deserved. They wanted to meet the "gardener touched with genius," as the great Dutch botanist, Hugo de Vries, described him.

Among his friends were Henry Ford, Thomas Edison, John Burroughs, John Muir, the King and Queen of Belgium, Paderewski, Harry Lauder, Schumann-Heink and countless others. Scientists, naturalists, musicians —all were welcome. But most welcome of all were the children of Santa Rosa.

Luther loved children, and they, in turn, loved and understood him. Though shy, he was always ready to talk to them. In his many talks in the schools, he always emphasized the importance of fairness, kindness, and hard work.

Arbor Day is the day on which children all over the United States plant trees. It is celebrated at different times in different states, depending on the climate. In California Arbor Day is known as Burbank Day. It is celebrated every year there on Luther Burbank's birthday, March 7.

On that day children of the town of Santa Rosa used to parade from their schools to his home to give him their birthday greetings. It was a great occasion for him as well as for them. They would wander with him through

his gardens and greenhouses, asking questions and admiring the flowers and fruits he had created.

These visits always ended with a short speech in which he never failed to talk to them about the wonderful world they lived in. He used to urge them to use their eyes and their ears in order not to miss a single bit of its beauty.

Luther loved his work and took pride in it. He believed that good work well done was sure to bring success and happiness. His enthusiasm, energy, and tireless patience had made the "impossible" possible. Hadn't he given perfume to scentless flowers, flavor to tasteless fruit, and brilliant color to dull-looking flowers? Hadn't he created fodder for cattle, fodder that could be grown on desert land?

It is almost impossible to believe that one man could accomplish as many "miracles" as Luther succeeded in doing. But what he did, he believed others could do. Though he had done so much, he felt that there was still much more that could be done. He hoped some of the youngsters to whom he talked might be influenced to go on with his work. He hoped some of them might want to explore a field in which they would add to the beauty and wealth of the world.

When Luther Burbank died in April, 1926, plant lovers all over the world mourned his passing. He had won a place in their hearts that no other could fill.

No wonder that Californians are proud of their Luther Burbank! No wonder this quiet, painstaking New Englander is remembered and honored throughout the world! To the world he is the green-thumbed wizard who created more plants and developed and improved more varieties than one can count. But to his friends and family he will always be remembered as the kind, warmhearted, understanding, and peace-loving "Uncle Lute."